TENNYSON'S CELEBRITY CIRCLE

BY CHARLOTTE BOYCE
& PÁRAIC FINNERTY

Tennyson's Celebrity Circle

Design © Roo Abrook
www.odysseygraphics.co.uk

Text © Charlotte Boyce and Páraic Finnerty

ISBN 9780956874368
Published 2011 by Tricorn Books,
a trading name of 131 Design Ltd
131 High Street, Old Portsmouth. PO1 2HW
www.tricornbooks.co.uk

University of Portsmouth

Contents

Victorian Celebrity

The concept of celebrity is one with which we are all too familiar in the twenty-first century; indeed, it is tempting to describe modern culture as celebrity-obsessed. But what is it that makes a 'celebrity'? Providing a definitive answer to this question proves a surprisingly tricky task. Celebrities are usually highly attractive and/or charismatic individuals who exist in the public domain. Although they may have a particular talent, often their gift is the art of getting noticed. Frequently, they crave public recognition and will do whatever it takes to get our attention. Sometimes, we are given so much intimate information about their lives that we may feel as though we are (unwittingly) stalking them! Yet it is not always certain why these individuals have been plucked from obscurity to become part of our daily consciousness or when they will be thrown back into the twilight world of the has-been or C-lister. A celebrity's longevity depends, to a large extent, on the Faustian pact he or she has implicitly made with the media. Newspapers, magazines, advertisements, films, television programmes and internet sites select which stars to promote and which to ditch carefully fashioning their choices to fit with the public's interests and concerns. The relationship between media and celebrity is a mutually beneficial though fragile one, usually lasting only until the latter falls from favour in scandalous circumstances or, in some cases, simply goes out of fashion.

We might assume that the cultural obsession with fame and stardom is a relatively recent phenomenon but, in fact, it dates back to the eighteenth century, when the word 'celebrity' came to describe not merely an attribute that one possessed but also an identity that was conferred on one by others. During this period, the figure of the celebrity became a recognisable social type, and a new relationship emerged between the person admired and his or her admirers. Out of this relationship, celebrity culture was born and it quickly set about transforming private individuals into public possessions.

During the Victorian period (1837-1901), the idealisation of celebrities was often indistinguishable from hero-worship, something for which this era had a strong propensity. 'Lionism' was the name given to the practice of bestowing cultural pre-eminence onto a person of note, while 'lionisers' were those who paid homage to (and often attempted to cultivate personal relationships with) the great men and women of the age. Whereas our modern celebrities tend to be actors, actresses, models and musicians, Victorian 'lions' were often artists, writers and poets. Victorian devotees would send these figures fan letters, collect their photographs and autographs, adopt their fashion or style, and even transform their homes and haunts into sites of pilgrimage. Put simply, Victorian fans coveted all objects, people and places associated with their heroes and heroines, and greedily consumed the latest news and gossip about their idols. Sound familiar?

Like today's media, Victorian newspapers and magazines worked hard to give readers the impression (or illusion) of real and unmediated contact with their favourite celebrities. Publishers, for instance, did everything they could to transform authors into figures with whom readers felt they had a material connection. This is typical of celebrity culture, which generates and encourages a pseudo-personal relationship between celebrity and fan, simulating a sense of interaction and shared experience even though, in most cases, the two parties have never actually met. If nineteenth-century readers believed that they had intimate access to their favourite authors, this could increase book sales, so the publishing industry coerced authors into catering for this belief. Commentators and critics who sought to detract attention from authors' personalities by focusing on the merits and erudite nature of their works ironically only increased the popularity and mass appeal of these figures.

The worship of celebrities in the Victorian period was facilitated by and inextricably linked to the rise of illustrated newspapers and magazines. These publications often featured engravings of famous faces, enabling readers to gain an accurate idea of what their idols looked like. New technologies, such as photography, similarly increased the visibility of Victorian celebrities, implicitly positioning them as objects of veneration, as well as of emotional and intellectual identification. The nineteenth century was

Tennyson's meeting with Italian revolutionary Giuseppe Garibaldi was front-page news in 1864. This illustration of the meeting appeared in the leading Victorian weekly newspaper the *Illustrated London News*.

also the age when biographies, autobiographies, celebrity letters and memoirs became marketable commodities, fuelled by the public's appetite for more and more information about (and new levels of access to) the lives of the famous. The gossip, rumours and anecdotes included in these texts, as well as in newspapers and magazines, not only helped to disseminate knowledge about celebrities but also made possible the pseudo-personal relationship between celebrity and fan mentioned above. In Victorian culture, celebrity became a public discourse in which the merits of individuals were debated and a consensus established, so that the worship of certain celebrities became virtually obligatory and a refusal to do so was taken as evidence of poor judgement or bad taste.

Some Victorian celebrities, like their modern-day equivalents, feared that they were becoming embroiled, internally and externally, in the celebrity machine and that any attempt to disentangle themselves or discover a 'self' uncontaminated by its workings was fruitless. This booklet tells the story of how the most famous poet of the Victorian period, Tennyson, attempted to extricate himself from his own celebrity and, in the process, created one of the most renowned celebrity circles of his age - a circle that included the most famous female photographer of the day, Julia Margaret Cameron; the most famous artist and sculptor, G. F. Watts; and two writers, Edward Lear and Lewis Carroll, who, although less well known at the time, later came to achieve a literary celebrity that is indisputable.

Alfred Tennyson

It is difficult from our twenty-first-century perspective to imagine a writer, not to mention a poet, enjoying the kind of adulation Alfred Tennyson (1809-92) experienced in the Victorian period. But in the years following his appointment as Poet Laureate in 1850 and until the time of his death in 1892, Tennyson was one of the most famous men in Britain; his renown and importance stretched across the British Empire and was strongly felt in the United States. A love and knowledge of Tennyson's poetry brought Britain together as a nation. Put simply, Tennyson was the most loved poet of his era and one of its A-list celebrities. One example of the devotion Tennyson inspired is afforded by the novelist and critic Edmund Gosse, who remembers his excitement at meeting Tennyson in 1871:

> Tennyson was scarcely a human being to us; he was the God of the Golden Bow; I approached him now like a blank idiot about to be slain [...] It is not merely that no person living now calls forth that kind of devotion, but the sentiment of mystery has disappeared.

Such adulation from a critic like Gosse explains why Tennyson was ranked alongside Spenser, Shakespeare, Milton and Byron as the greatest of British poets.

From the 1850s onwards Tennyson's celebrity was vigorously promoted by his publishers who underlined his position as the nation's poet, and presented him as one of the representative men of the age, whose works reflected its anxieties, passions and thoughts. Not only was his poetry celebrated and praised by critics, and a source of inspiration for poets, novelists and artists, it was also commercially successful and read by the general public. Ordinary people knew Tennyson's poems by heart and they transformed him into a venerated and revered sage. In addition, his image - reproduced in paintings, engravings and photographs - made him one of the most recognisable figures of the day.

Particularly in the 1840s and 1850s, Tennyson, anxious to support himself and later his family, engaged in strategic self-promotion to secure and increase the readership of his poems. For example, he allowed poems to appear in gift books and magazines, despite his personal dislike of these popular forms. However, he remained suspicious of 'celebrity'. Tennyson's most explicit attack on the cult of fame is his poem 'To ------ After Reading a Life and Letters,' first published in *The Examiner* in 1849. In this poem, he expresses his disgust at the recent publication of the love letters of John Keats, arguing that a poet should cultivate privacy and live an unrecorded life:

You might have won the Poet's name,
If such be worth the winning now,
And gained a laurel for your brow
Of sounder leaf than I can claim;

But you have made the wiser choice,
A life that moves to gracious ends
Through troops of unrecording friends,
A deedful life, a silent voice;

And you have missed the irreverent doom
Of those that wear the Poet's crown;
Hereafter neither knave nor clown
Shall hold their orgies at your tomb.

For now the Poet cannot die,
Nor leave his music as of old,
But round him, ere he scarce be cold,
Begins the scandal and the cry:

"Proclaim the faults he would not show;
Break lock and seal; betray the trust;
Keep nothing sacred; 'tis but just
The many-headed beast should know."

Ah, shameless! For he did but sing
A song that pleased us from its worth;
No public life was his on earth,
No blazoned statesman he, nor king.

He gave the people of his best;
His worst he kept, his best he gave.
My Shakespeare's curse on clown and knave
Who will not let his ashes rest!

Who make it seem more sweet to be
The little life of bank and brier,
The bird that pipes his lone desire
And dies unheard within his tree,

That he that warbles long and loud
And drops at Glory's temple-gates,
For whom the carrion vulture waits
To tear his heart before the crowd!

According to the poem, the unrecognised, unknown poet is better off because he or she avoids the 'irreverent doom' of publicity and the personal intrusion to which the public believes it has a right. This poem explains why Tennyson was at first so reluctant to take on the very public role of Poet Laureate when it was offered to him. Tennyson hated the celebrity-driven invasiveness of Victorian culture.

In each of the years following his appointment as Poet Laureate, Tennyson increasingly grew to dislike his own fame and the way his celebrity seemed to give others permission to violate his personal space. In his reminiscence of Tennyson, Frederick Locker-Lampson recalls:

> Tennyson says that as a boy he had a great thirst to be a poet, and to be a popular poet. He would rove through the fields composing hundreds of couplets, and shouting them to the skies; but that now he is inclined to think popularity is a bastard fame, which sometimes goes with the more real thing, but is independent of and somewhat antagonistic to it. He appears to shrink from his own popularity. He maintains that the artist should spare no pains, that he should do his very best for the sake of his art, and for that only.

Fame asked too much of Tennyson, a sensitive, shy man, who became paranoid and obsessive about protecting his privacy. When he stayed at a hotel he signed the register on his departure for fear that he would be mobbed by admirers, and he was so wary of his letters being sold to the highest bidder that he often disguised his handwriting. Moreover, he became careful about his possessions, knowing that enthusiasts sought any objects associated with or used by him, for example, an autograph, a letter, the tea cup or saucer he used, or even a strand of his hair. Aware of the 'Tennyson effect', advertisers sometimes used his name without permission to endorse and increase the sales of products such as fountain pens and pills for constipation. Tennyson hated all of this, but was most riled by the way in which newspapers made up lies about him, presenting him as cantankerous and eccentric, and on one occasion even going so far as to suggest that he took opium. Years later, he told his daughter-in-law, Audrey Tennyson, that he was 'sick of this publicity - all this fullsome [sic] adulation makes me miserable and inclined to vomit morally... most of the things said about me in the papers are lies, lies, lies.'

Tennyson nicknamed this photograph of himself, taken by Julia Margaret Cameron in 1865, 'The Dirty Monk'. It was to remain one of the Laureate's favourite images of himself.

This photograph of Alfred and Emily Tennyson and their sons, Hallam and Lionel, standing outside their home, was taken by the pioneering Swedish photographer Oscar Gustave Rejlander, who visited Freshwater in 1863.

In the years following his laureateship, Tennyson felt bombarded by admirers and no longer able to protect himself and his family from the invasion of unannounced visitors at Chapel House, his Twickenham home. The poet decided, in 1853, that they should leave London and relocate to Freshwater, a remote region of the Isle of Wight, believing that here they could enjoy a quiet life away from his admirers, seeing only their friends, at the times of their choosing. The family moved into Farringford House on 25 November 1853 and rented it until Tennyson had sufficient money, in 1856, to purchase it outright. The house was on a sizable estate described by its visitors as a place of seclusion and simplicity, where as one observer put it, 'every tree that grew had felt a kind of personal responsibility to keep the intruder out.'

For almost forty years, Tennyson, his wife, Emily, and their sons, Hallam and Lionel, entertained guests at Farringford. Although Tennyson had sought isolation, his wife knew that he would also miss his friends and become bored of his new restricted life, so she ensured that they had a steady stream of guests at their home. Moreover, Tennyson's status as Poet Laureate attracted some of the most admired figures of the nineteenth century to the Isle of Wight, including Henry Wadsworth Longfellow, Aubrey de Vere, John Everett Millais, Algernon Charles Swinburne, Ellen Terry, William Holman Hunt, Coventry Patmore, Tom Taylor, Charles Kingsley, the Duke and Duchess of Argyll, and Giuseppe Garibaldi. While Edward Lear and Lewis Carroll were frequent visitors to Freshwater, Julia Margaret Cameron and G.F. Watts enjoyed their visits so much that they decided to become residents there.

Many of these visitors left records of their time at Farringford and these reminiscenses were published in Hallam Tennyson's two-volume *Alfred Lord Tennyson, A Memoir by His Son* (1897) or elsewhere. Rumours of Tennyson's reclusiveness, rudeness and vanity are substantiated by some of his guests, but others remember his charm and cordiality; the poet is described as displaying shyness and reserve, but also hospitality and friendliness. Guests recall conversations over dinner about Yarmouth pier or Lincolnshire; singing, piano-playing and performances in private theatricals; dessert being served in the drawing room; pipe-smoking in the attic with the poet; Tennyson's complaints about magazines; and his after-dinner readings of his most famous poems, new compositions and works-in-progress (whether guests wanted to hear them or not). What visitors to Farringford gained was an intimate portrait of one of the most famous men of the day and they expressed their feelings of privilege at being given the opportunity to know and understand him. Other guests remember accompanying Tennyson on his daily two-hour walk on the High Down (later called Tennyson Down). Reflecting on this, Anne Thackeray Ritchie, the daughter of the novelist William Makepeace Thackeray, wrote the following to Tennyson:

> Who knows perhaps, when we are all peacefully together again, (and I always think of old days on Freshwater downs as the nearest thing to heaven I ever could imagine), you will still walk ahead and point to the sea and to the sky, and touch things and make them shine for us and flash into our hearts, as you have ever done.

Emily Tennyson began sitting for G.F. Watts in November 1862 and the resulting portrait is the only representation of her that adequately captures the gentle and ethereal nature of this shy and retiring woman.

Emily Tennyson

If Tennyson's guests enjoyed their time at Farringford then this was largely due to Tennyson's wife, Emily. When Emily Sellwood (1813-1896) eventually married Tennyson on 13 June 1850, after a lengthy engagement and even a break-up, she married a promising poet; however, after they returned from their honeymoon in October 1850, owing to the immense success of *In Memoriam* (1850), Emily found herself married to the most sought-after poet of the day, whose celebrity was on a par with that of Dickens. Emily disliked publicity perhaps even more so than her husband and was glad that he was protective of their domestic and intimate life, and never mentioned her in his poetry. She was happy when her husband suggested that they move to Freshwater and never worried about its isolation. On first looking from the drawing-room window at Farringford, Emily thought 'I must have that view' and came to regard their home as the 'dearest place on earth'.

However, the volume of visitors over the years meant that Emily felt as if she were running a hotel, in addition to being Tennyson's business manager and secretary. As well as the practicalities of having guests, Emily had to protect her husband from overbearing ones, while ensuring that all their visitors were comfortable and happy. While Tennyson had a tendency to bouts of unsociability, his wife was always the perfect hostess, despite her own ill-health. Emily made friends with her visitors and became a very important figure in their lives beyond Freshwater. The visitor Emily grew closest to was Edward Lear, with whom she exchanged intimate letters in which she encouraged his creativity and countered his self-doubts about his art and his social skills. Lear was one of the figures to whom Emily confided about the strain placed on her by having so many visitors at Farringford. Julia Margaret Cameron also greatly esteemed Emily, regarding her as a 'living stream of love whose fount is never dry' and often visited Farringford to spend time with Emily when Tennyson was away. The poet Aubrey De Vere said of Emily:

...She is a woman full of soul as well as mind, and in all her affections, it seems to me that it is in the soul, and for the soul, that she loves those dear to her. [...] I regard her as one of the 'few noble' whom it has been my lot to meet in life [...] She is a person to whom you will be greatly drawn whenever you are near her...

In addition, Emily encouraged Tennyson in his associations with artists and painters such as Millais and Watts. Often the Tennysons' mutual friends turned to her when they had a request for her husband, hoping she would intercede. For example, in 1862, when Watts wanted copies of his portrait of Tennyson autographed by the poet, he asked Emily rather than her husband. What very few people beyond the Isle of Wight circle knew about was Emily's talent for music, and that she composed musical settings for her husband's poems. It was only after his death that her compositions were published.

Between 1857 and 1890, G. F. Watts painted six portraits of Tennyson; in this 1863/4 painting, Tennyson is depicted in front of laurel leaves, which symbolise poetic greatness and inspiration.

Tourism

At first, Freshwater offered its residents and visitors a calm and serene place where poetry and creativity could flourish, a place beyond the prying eyes of the world. But from the 1860s onwards this Eden began to change. In 1860, Emily told her friend Margaret Getty that she wanted to leave Freshwater because 'this place is becoming far too public for us'. On one level, this was because more and more houses were being built around Farringford, but also because of the influx of tourists to the Isle of Wight, particularly in the summer months. In an 1860 letter to her husband, Julia Margaret Cameron explains exactly the effect of this on Freshwater's reclusive poet:

> The visitors look at him. Tourists seek him. Americans visit him. Ladies pester and pursue him. Enthusiasts dun him for a bit of stone off his gate. These things make life a burden, and his great soul suffers from these [illegible] stings ... The looking at him would be the most capital offence of all if he were Ruler of the Universe. And yet he is so worth looking at: so grand in form and character, and even in his shrinking there is a sad and serious helplessness - and no offensiveness. [...]

William Holman Hunt was told by Tennyson that once when he was gardening he heard a voice shout 'There he is – look' and was then confronted by half a dozen admirers staring fixedly at him, and that on another occasion a more daring intruder flattened his nose against the window of the house, crying 'You can see him well from here'.

Of course, one of the reasons Freshwater became a tourist resort was because it was a haven of celebrities, and visitors came to catch a glimpse of these figures, encouraged by guidebooks to the island and local newspapers, which announced the arrivals and departures of public figures and celebrities and the hotels at which they stayed. Hester Fuller, Thackeray's granddaughter, recalls, 'People walking in the lanes would stop to watch them pass, and a visitor to Freshwater was heard pathetically exclaiming "Is there no one who is commonplace here? Is everybody either a poet, or a genius, or a painter, or peculiar in some way?"' Most of the guidebooks to the Isle of Wight, including those owned by the Tennysons, refer to Farringford as 'hallowed ground' and a shrine to the poet, noting also that the locals were in awe of and respectful towards their Poet Laureate neighbour, whom, they believed, wrote poems while mowing the lawn.

Often these guidebooks quote some of the lines from Tennyson's poem 'To the Rev, F. D. Maurice' (1854), which invited Hallam's godfather to Farringford:

> Come, when no graver cares employ,
> Godfather, come and see your boy:
> Your presence will be sun in winter,
> Making the little one leap for joy. [...]
>
> Where, far from noise and smoke of town,
> I watch the twilight falling brown
> All round a careless-order'd garden
> Close to the ridge of a noble down.
>
> You'll have no scandal while you dine,
> But honest talk and wholesome wine,
> And only hear the magpie gossip
> Garrulous under a roof of pine:
>
> For groves of pine on either hand,
> To break the blast of winter, stand;
> And further on, the hoary Channel
> Tumbles a billow on chalk and sand. [...]
>
> Come, Maurice, come: the lawn as yet
> Is hoar with rime, or spongy-wet;
> But when the wreath of March has blossom'd
> Crocus, anemone, violet,
>
> Or later, pay one visit here,
> For those are few we hold as dear:
> Nor pay but one, but come for many,
> Many and many a happy year.

It seems as if tourists interpreted the poem as a personal invitation from Tennyson to visit him, whereas in reality he viewed tourists as 'inquisitive sightseers' and later guidebooks warned visitors that their obtrusive presence was driving the poet from the island:

> Most people who visit Freshwater ask for the house of the poet. It is so buried in trees that it cannot be seen except by trespassing, of which it is said the poet so bitterly complains that he had it some time since in contemplation to quit the island.

This 1864 illustration of the south side of Farringford House was done by Edward Lear, one of the Tennysons' most frequent guests. A compulsive wanderer, who often experienced feelings of intense loneliness, Lear described Farringford as one of his favourite places on earth.

During the Victorian period, Freshwater became a popular tourist destination; many visitors travelled there hoping to catch a glimpse one of the village's famous inhabitants.

George G. Napier notes in *The Homes and Haunts of Alfred Lord Tennyson* (1892): 'Now that (Tennyson's) fame encircled the globe, Farringford became one of the most overrun spots in Europe, people lurking about the shrubberies, staring in at his windows, and watching him as he walked out of his gates.' Often guidebooks drew attention to Tennyson's right to privacy, adding further to gossip about his reclusiveness, while at the same time highlighting the location of his residence for celebrity hunters. While the adulation Tennyson experienced must have appealed to his vanity, he hated the way the Isle of Wight was being invaded by 'Cockneys' - Tennyson's derisive and contemptuous appellation for the celebrity-obsessed nuisances who disturbed his peace. Once the short-sighted poet fled before the approach of a flock of sheep thinking it was a group of tourists. Such anecdotes about Tennyson's paranoia have ensured that this has become part of the poet's posthumous reputation. Looking back on the 1850s the *Southern Evening Echo* in 1969 recorded the following:

> the crowds would gather in the shaded lane that separated (Farringford) house from the farm in order to see Tennyson walk on to High Down. To retain his privacy he had built a rustic bridge over the lane. It was to little avail. The people now collected beneath it in the hope of catching a glimpse of the Laureate hurrying across in his military cloak, with his big hat pulled down over his tangled hair.

Of course, the more Tennyson retreated from the public eye and fashioned himself as the cloistered poet, the more intriguing he became to his admirers. In addition, Tennyson's celebrity transformed a calm, rural setting, where he initially went to get away from celebrity culture, into a tourist attraction. By the 1860s, Tennyson grew so wary of venturing outside his own door during the summer months that he and his family frequently left the island, holidaying in France or visiting Grayshott or London. Of one such location, a cautious Tennyson told a friend:

> I don't give the name of the place (where we are staying) because I wish it to be kept secret: I am not flying from the cockneys here to tumble in among the cockneys there I hope: tho' some of my friends assert that it will be so...

From 1869, having purchased Aldworth House, near Haslemere, Tennyson and his family made this, rather than Farringford, their summer residence.

Yet despite all of this the Isle of Wight was a conducive place for Tennyson's creativity and it was here that he wrote some of his most famous poems, including *Maud* (1855), *Idylls of the King* (1859 -1885) and *Enoch Arden* (1864). Tennyson often read the poems he was working on to his guests, believing that this helped his composition. Of course, each of these poems and in particular *Idylls of the King* increased Tennyson's popularity and fortune. In addition, his interactions with the other literary and artistic celebrities he attracted to the island fostered collaborations and artistic inspiration. Tennyson was painted, sculpted and photographed, and his poems inspired illustrations, photographs and music. These artworks not only increased Tennyson's fame, making his one of the most recognisable faces of the Victorian period, they increased Watt's fame and made Cameron a celebrity in her own right.

Julia Margaret Cameron

When, in 1874, Tennyson suggested to his close friend and Freshwater neighbour, Julia Margaret Cameron (1815 -1879), that she produce a series of photographic illustrations for his poetic epic, *Idylls of the King*, she responded with customary enthusiasm: 'Now you know, Alfred, that I know that it is immortality to me to be bound up with you.' As Cameron recognised, any kind of public affiliation with the internationally renowned Poet Laureate could only serve to enhance her own growing reputation as a photographer. However, it would also be fair to say that Tennyson's 'immortalisation' in Victorian culture owed much to his relationship with Cameron. The Laureate may have been the leading luminary of the Freshwater circle, but Julia Margaret Cameron was its driving social force and, by means of her distinctive, full-head photographic portraits, she helped to cement the fame of the various literary, artistic and scientific greats who congregated around her home and studio on the Isle of Wight.

During the Victorian era, the public appetite for celebrity photographs was huge. Images of famous figures were reprinted and sold in vast numbers, usually in the form of pocket-sized cartes-de-visites, which could be collected and arranged into albums (Cameron herself often presented such albums as gifts to her friends and relatives). Having taken up photography relatively late in life (her first camera was presented to her as a Christmas gift in 1863), Cameron found herself ideally placed to take advantage of the Victorian vogue for celebrity portraits. While living in London in the 1850s, she had been a regular visitor to the literary and artistic salon established at Little Holland House by her sister, the redoubtable Sara Prinsep, and it was here that she encountered many of the eminent figures who would later be persuaded to sit before her lens: the painters G.F. Watts and William Holman Hunt, the actress Ellen Terry, the historian Thomas Carlyle, the poet and playwright Sir Henry Taylor and, of course, the Laureate, Alfred Tennyson. As an 1866 review of Cameron's work pointed out, 'her position in literary and aristocratic society gives her the pick of the most beautiful and intellectual heads in the world.'

Cameron's successes were attributable as much to her tenacious personality as they were to her social position, however. Her powers of persuasion were such that even the reluctant Tennyson found himself submitting obediently to her will; she mischievously described one of her most famous portraits of him, 'The Dirty Monk', as 'a column of immortal grandeur - done by my will against his.' He, in turn, described her sitters as her 'victims', once warning the American poet, Henry Wadsworth Longfellow, 'you will have to do whatever she tells you. I'll come back soon and see what is left of you.' Cameron's relatives, likewise, described her as a formidable, if rather eccentric, woman. According to her great-niece, Laura Gurney (later Lady Troubridge),

> Aunt Julia appeared as a terrifying elderly woman, short and squat...dressed in dark clothes, stained with chemicals from her photography (and smelling of them, too) with a plump eager face and piercing eyes, and a voice husky and a little harsh, yet in some way compelling and even charming.

Recalling the childhood experience of being made to pose as an angel, 'scantily clad' and with 'heavy swan's wings' fastened to her shoulders, Gurney wrote, 'No wonder those old photographs...look anxious and wistful. This is how we felt, for we never knew what Aunt Julia was going to do next, nor did anyone else.' Tennyson's friend Benjamin Jowett suggested that Cameron had 'a tendency to make the house shake the moment she [entered]' -though, he added kindly, 'in this dull world that is a very excusable fault.' Tennyson seems to have shared Jowett's opinion for, although the endlessly energetic Cameron denied him the peace and quiet that he craved, constantly pestering him with requests for photographs and autographs and handwritten copies of his work, he was very fond of her and, along with his wife and sons, spent much time in her family's company.

This 1874 photograph by Julia Margaret Cameron was designed to illustrate one of Tennyson's poems, 'The May Queen'. The model, Emily Peacock, features in a number of Cameron's photographs.

Although a keen photographer of others, Cameron disliked having her own picture taken. In this image, dated c.1858, she is shown with two of her sons, Charles Hay Cameron and Henry Herschel Hay Cameron.

This famous 1865 photograph by Cameron is titled 'The Whisper of th Muse'. It features G. F. Watts as a musician and two Freshwater girls Kate and Elizabeth Keown, as his muses.

The Camerons had moved to the Isle of Wight in 1860, choosing to settle in a property adjoining the Farringford estate which they christened 'Dimbola' after one of the family's coffee plantations in Ceylon (now Sri Lanka). Their arrival had a considerable impact on life in the Tennyson household. Cameron, renowned for her extravagant generosity, would often turn up, unannounced, arms laden with gifts. Shortly after moving in to Dimbola, she presented a somewhat bemused Emily with two legs of Welsh mutton and several rolls of vivid blue wallpaper emblazoned with a border from the Elgin Marbles. The Tennysons' protestations against these acts of benevolence had little effect: when, a couple of months later, the poet Edward Lear came to stay at Farringford, Cameron arranged for her grand piano to be hauled over from Dimbola so that Lear could perform musical versions of Tennyson's poems after dinner. (The gesture was well-meant but, as we shall see, alienated Lear, who found Cameron's exuberance too overbearing.)

Following the Camerons' arrival in Freshwater, Dimbola quickly became the social hub of the village: the inhabitants of Little Holland House were frequent visitors, as were Sir Henry Taylor and his family and, of course, the Tennysons (a special gate was even installed at the back of the grounds so that Tennyson could walk between Farringford and Dimbola unharassed by pesky members of the public). Guests were invariably inveigled into participating in the constant stream of activities organised by Cameron. Some, like Taylor, found themselves dressed up in elaborate costumes and made to pose for photographic interpretations of famous scenes from Shakespearean drama or Tennysonian verse; others, like young Hallam and Lionel Tennyson, found themselves with starring roles in the amateur theatricals that were regularly staged at Dimbola's purpose-built 'Thatched House Theatre'. Local people were also coerced into sitting for Cameron: William Warder, a Yarmouth porter, was selected to pose as King Arthur in the series of photographs illustrating Tennyson's *Idylls of the King*, while, in the famous image 'The Whisper of the Muse,' two Freshwater girls, Kate and Elizabeth Keown, appear alongside Watts.

Given its inhabitants' unwavering focus on artistic pursuits, it is perhaps unsurprising to discover that Dimbola was a fairly shambolic household. Two of Cameron's maids, Mary Hillier (a local girl) and Mary Ryan (an Irish beggar girl rescued by Cameron from the London streets) were also her favourite models and, consequently, seem to have spent more time posing for photographs than doing housework. The preparation of meals was certainly not a priority at Dimbola: Anne Thackeray Ritchie, a regular visitor, affectionately remembered eating nothing but bacon and eggs for breakfast, lunch and dinner during one of her stays there. As the poet William Allingham observed, rather disapprovingly, 'Mrs C. and her household take no note of time.' Indeed, Dimbola seems to have been given over entirely to the rather messy art of photography. As Cameron herself admitted in her posthumously published

autobiography, '[My] habit of running into the dining room with my wet pictures has stained such an immense quantity of table linen with nitrate of silver, indelible stains, that I should have been banished from any less indulgent household.' The chemicals used by Cameron in the developing process also tended to stain her person; when she was introduced to the celebrated Italian revolutionary Garibaldi at Farringford in 1864, he initially thought she was a beggar-woman, so black were her hands.

It was out of this chaotic domestic environment that Cameron managed to produce some of the most striking images of the Victorian age. Although a number of her contemporaries were critical of her unfocused, life-sized heads and baffled by her refusal to retouch her work, others championed her artistic vision. Watts, in particular, admired her approach (which was influenced in no small measure by his own painterly style): he labelled her photographs 'quite divine' and wrote under one, 'I wish I could paint a picture such as this.' Cameron sought to distinguish herself from the purely commercial portrait photographers of her day, who tended to arrange their subjects in a series of stock poses and produce sharply focused but rather dull images. She wasn't interested in scientific exactitude, writing instead of her desire 'to ennoble Photography and to secure for it the character and uses of High Art by combining the real and Ideal and sacrificing nothing of Truth by all possible devotion to Poetry and beauty.' This commitment to 'combining the real and Ideal' can be seen in her photographs of nineteenth-century male celebrities, such as Tennyson, Watts, Carlyle, Sir John Herschel (the renowned astronomer) and Charles Darwin. Softly focused and dramatically lit, these images aimed to capture not only the appearance of the sitter but also those less tangible qualities that contributed to his fame. 'When I have had such men before my camera my whole soul has endeavoured to do its duty towards them in recording faithfully the greatness of the inner as well as the features of the outer man,' Cameron explained in her autobiography.

Yet, for all her commitment to photography as an art-form, Cameron was also commercially aware: as well as being one of the first photographers to copyright her images, she also organised a number of exhibitions to promote her work and coaxed friends into writing positive reviews. In 1864, she entered into a formal agreement with London's leading printsellers, P. & D. Colnaghi, for the sale and distribution of her pictures; ten years later, she engaged the Autotype Company to produce and sell new carbon prints of seventy of her best-known works. Photography was an expensive business and, as Cameron readily acknowledged, she needed to recoup her costs. In order to maximise the commercial value of her portraits, she badgered famous friends such as Tennyson and Herschel to autograph them; 'your name would justly add enormously to my reputation and thus greatly quicken the sale of my photographs - which is for me most needful now,' she once wrote cajolingly to Herschel. Tennyson, unsurprisingly, hated signing pictures of himself, but capitulated in the face of Cameron's demands. One of the downsides of doing so, however, was that his image became more widely circulated and his face increasingly recognisable to his fans. He would often grumble to Cameron about the subsequent loss of privacy: 'I can't go anonymous by reason of your confounded photographs.'

If Cameron's photographs helped to immortalise the members of her circle, they were also instrumental in securing her own fame. It is clear that she was keen to make a name for herself both among fellow artists and the general public and, in this respect, her attitude to 'celebrity' seems to have been less ambivalent than that of some of her peers. She embraced public acclaim. Emily Tennyson recalled her proudly reporting the way in which she had been feted during a visit to Oxford: 'She says that the Poet Laureate could not have had more honour paid him at Oxford than she had.' Cameron's autobiography suggests a similar sense of pride in her achievements: referring to the reception of the works she contributed to the 1865 Exhibition of the Photographic Society of Scotland, she wrote:

> Artists...immediately crowned me with laurels, and though 'Fame' is pronounced 'The last infirmity of noble minds,' I must confess that when those whose judgement I revered have valued and praised my works, 'my heart has leapt up like a rainbow in the sky,' and I have renewed my zeal.

Unfortunately, Cameron's career as a photographer was hindered by her family's return to Ceylon in 1875. The hot climate was not conducive to the photographic process and, though she continued to take pictures during her time there, her Ceylonese images failed to achieve the renown of those produced during her years at Freshwater. Nevertheless, Cameron remained committed to her artistic ideals until her death in 1879: fittingly, her final word, as she gazed out on the Ceylonese landscape, was reported to have been 'Beautiful.'

G.F. Watts and Ellen Terry

At the time of his death, G.F. Watts (1817-1904) had created some of the most famous sculptures and paintings of the Victorian era, and had become known as the 'English Michelangelo'. According to his wife Mary, at the end of his life he shared Tennyson's opinion that 'in these days too much is written of every one who comes at all before the public', and he envied 'the oblivion that now hides every fact of the life of the man whose name stands first in literature (meaning Shakespeare)'. Yet owing to his humble origins, in his early career Watts was determined to gain fame and recognition as an artist. He attended the Royal Academy and had his work exhibited there in 1837, after which he secured patronage and began to make a living from his artworks. The subsequent recognition he achieved in the 1840s meant that by 1850 he had attracted the attention of one of the great lionisers of the period, Sara Prinsep. Sara and her husband, Henry Thoby, invited him to become a permanent resident at their home, Little Holland House, Kensington, where he lived and worked for the next two decades. Mrs Prinsep's circle included some of the most distinguished and eminent

In this 1879 self-portrait, G.F. Watts wears a skullcap to associate himself and his work with the sixteenth-century Italian artist Titian.

figures of the period, including William Gladstone, Benjamin Disraeli, William Holman Hunt, Edward Burne-Jones, Thomas Carlyle, John Ruskin and Charles Dickens. Rather than collecting paintings or books, she collected artists, writers and intellectuals and exhibited them in her salon. It was among this cosmopolitan and bohemian coterie that Watts first met those who would become part of the Isle of Wight's equivalent cultural and literary circle: Julia Margaret Cameron, Tennyson and Ellen Terry.

It was around this time that Watts decided to concentrate on portrait painting and set himself the task of depicting the most eminent figures of the age and placing these images in a collection he called the 'Hall of Fame'. Watts viewed his task as a form of public service and over his lifetime he aimed to capture not merely the profiles of these figures but their very souls. His 'Hall of Fame' included John Everett Millais, Matthew Arnold, Henry Edward Manning, Cecil John Rhodes, John Stuart Mill, William Morris, Thomas Carlyle, Algernon Charles Swinburne and Robert Browning. Watts gave this collection of portraits to the newly established National Portrait Gallery, which still displays some of them, while the others are exhibited in Bodelwyddan Castle in North Wales. One of the paintings in this collection is Watt's 1864 portrait of Tennyson.

Tennyson and Watts first met in 1858 in Little Holland House and in November of that year Watts finished his first portrait of Tennyson—he would go on to paint Tennyson another five times. Watts became a frequent visitor to Freshwater, usually staying at Dimbola; in 1862 he painted a portrait of Emily and later, in 1865, one of Tennyson and his sons, which he gave to the poet as a sign of their friendship and a token of his respect and reverence. If Watts was inspired by Tennyson, Tennyson was greatly interested in Watts's opinions on art, although he didn't always agree with him. Tennyson recorded Watts's ideas about portrait painting in these lines from *Idylls of the King*:

> As when a painter, poring on a face,
> Divinely thro' all hindrance finds the man
> Behind it, and so paints him that his face,
> The shape and colour of a mind and life,
> Lives for his children, ever at best.

This portrait of Ellen Terry, entitled *Choosing*, was completed by G.F. Watts in 1864, the year that she gave up her career on the stage to marry him; after their marriage, the couple spent their honeymoon in Freshwater.

Watts also gave Julia Margaret Cameron advice on how to get her sitters to pose, and, in turn, learnt from Cameron about photography and often used photographs to inspire his painting. In addition, they shared models, one of whom, Ellen Terry (1847-1928), would go on to become one of the most famous actresses of the Victorian age.

In 1862, Watts met Terry and her sister Kate at Little Holland House and in the same year they sat for his painting *The Sisters*. Watts and Terry married two years later, on 20 February 1864, despite the thirty-year age difference between them. Watts said that he married Terry, who had recently launched her adult theatrical career, to save her from the corruption of the stage. They spent their honeymoon at Dimbola, where they travelled accompanied by the Prinseps. Terry was a model for Watts's paintings *Choosing* (1864) and *Ophelia* (1864), and while in Freshwater she posed for photographs by Cameron, including one entitled *Sadness* (1864). To escape the oppressive adult company at Dimbola, Terry often went to Farringford to play Knights of the Round Table with Tennyson's sons. While there, she also enjoyed conversations with Tennyson, learnt how to prepare his pipe and accompanied him on his daily walks on the Downs; it was on these walks that he taught her the names of flowers and birds.

The marriage between Watts and Terry was over within a year, not only because of the age difference but also because of the interference of Mrs Prinsep, who was always reprimanding Terry and commenting on her behaviour. The marriage caused a degree of scandal and became a source of celebrity gossip. As the critic Nina Auerbach has noted:

> During its short life...the marriage exuded hints of intrigue, obscenity, even perversity. At their weekly dinner, the editors of *Punch* amused each other by exchanging ribald speculations about it. There was something lip-smacking in the idea of quivering old men - and the frail hypochondriac Watts looked even older than he was - violating beautiful children.

By being the muse for Watts's paintings and Cameron's photographs Terry gained a public profile that facilitated her subsequent success as an actress. After Ellen Terry became famous, journalists accused Watts of violating and spoiling her innocence, even though it was Watts's paintings of Terry that connected her with ingenuousness in the public's imagination. Such vilification of Watts was exacerbated by the kind of enthusiastic devotion a celebrity actress inspired. Audience members, sitting in the darkened theatres, believed that performers were speaking directly to them, and these same viewers wanted access to the private lives of actors and actresses, lives which were so completely hidden by the roles that they played.

In 1872, Tennyson suggested that Watts move to Freshwater and by the end of 1873 the Briary was built and became a home for Watts and the Prinseps, who had lost much of their fortune owing to the failure of the coffee crop in Ceylon. Freshwater now had three celebrity houses, creating, as Edmund Gosse noted, 'a splendid exclusive society which circled more or less round Tennyson'—a coterie caught up in 'a radiance of mutual admiration'. Although Tennyson may have been the centre of the attention Watts and Cameron were also lures for the celebrity seekers and tourists. Yet for those within the circle fame may have seemed commonplace. For example, when Tennyson's grandnieces, Laura and Blanche, were misbehaving in Watts's studio, Emily told them that 'he was a great man, and a celebrity'. Interestingly, the girls reflected that this 'conveyed nothing to us, and as he had none of the airs of either, the fact of his genius, if we thought of it at all, seemed like something belonging specially to us.'

If Tennyson's grandnieces were less than impressed by celebrity or genius it might have been a result of its abundance in the Freshwater vicinity, or it might reflect their granduncle's hostility to fame. Interestingly, Watts told Tennyson that intrusions on one's privacy were the 'cost of fame', to which Tennyson responded: 'I wish I had never written a line in my life', only to be remonstrated by his friend: 'Ah, now you would not have made your Arthur speak like that!' After Tennyson's death, Watts began work on a huge bronze sculpture of the poet for the grounds of Lincoln Cathedral; this was a personal labour to honour his beloved friend, and was erected a year after Watts's death.

Edward Lear

At the moment he entered Tennyson's celebrity circle, Edward Lear (1812-1888) was primarily known as a traveller and illustrator. He had so impressed Queen Victoria with his illustrations that she invited him to Buckingham Palace, in 1846, to give her drawing lessons. However, for much of his life, Lear remained an eccentric outsider, a man less than comfortable in his own skin or in the company of others. Lear's literary fame was a posthumous one and rests today on his invention of nonsense verse and poems such as 'The Owl and Pussycat' (1867). As a result, Lear, like Carroll, was not a Victorian celebrity but instead would become one, and like Carroll, he was not photographed by Cameron or painted by Watts.

In 1851, Lear was introduced to the Tennysons by one of their mutual friends, Franklin Lushington. A little while after this meeting, Lear sent the couple a copy of his two-volume *Journal of a Landscape Painter in Greece and Albania* (1851) as a belated wedding present. Tennyson admired the work and wrote 'To E.L. on his Travels in Greece', the following lines of which are printed on Lear's tombstone in the cemetery in San Remo:

> all things fair,
> With such a pencil, such a pen,
> You shadow forth to distant men,
> I read and felt that I was there:

Even before his meeting with Tennyson, Lear greatly admired the poet and it was his lifelong ambition to illustrate his poems. Although Tennyson and Lear respected each other's work, they never had a close friendship. In one of his early letters to Tennyson, Lear confided: 'I feel woundily like a spectator - all though my life - of what goes on amongst those I know'.

In 1854 Emily invited Lear to spend Christmas at Farringford. He did not accept this invitation but, in the summer of 1855, he wrote to Tennyson to ask if he might stay near them, requesting 'a big room looking to the North? - so that I could paint in it quietly, & come & see you & Mrs. Tennyson promiscuously?' However, it was not until October 1855 that he first visited Farringford, accompanied by his friend Lushington. During his stay, Emily recorded in her journal the delight that everyone took in Lear when he put musical settings to and sang Tennyson's poems: 'Mariana,' 'The Lotus Eaters,' 'Ellen Adair,' 'Tears idle tears,' 'Let the solid ground' and 'O that 'twere possible.'

In a letter written to Emily shortly after his first visit, Lear expressed his great love for the place and its residents:

> Not but what I have thought of Faringford [sic] at all times & seasons ever since I left. In the morning I see everything - even to the plate of Mushrooms: then Hallam & Lionel come in, - & when they are gone, you, Alfred & Frank begin to talk like Gods together careless of mankind: - & so on, all through the day... I really do believe that I enjoy hardly any one thing on earth while it is present: - always looking back, or frettingly peering into the dim beyond. With all this, I may say to you and Alfred, that the 3 or 4 days of the 16th-20th. October/55, were the best I have passed for many a long day. If I live to grow old, & can hope to exist in England, I should like to be somewhere near you in one's later days.

Lear told her, 'Forgetting you or Alfred or Faringford [sic] is always a fiddlededeeism & impossible' and emphasised his longing to return to this joyous place: 'I do wish I could be at (or near—not at) Faringford for a while.' Lear took great pleasure in his subsequent visits to Farringford in 1857 and 1859, when he sang, went on walks with Tennyson and heard the poet reading his poems. On one of these occasions, Edith Nicholl Ellison remembers that Lear invented a musical setting for Tennyson's *Maud* (1855) and that the poet was 'charmed, and marched up and down the room, occasionally adding his own voice to that of the singer, and exclaiming, "Lear, you have revealed more of my Maud to myself!"' And in 1859, Lear published musical settings to poems from *Idylls of the King* and a collection of settings to Tennyson's earlier poems. It is little wonder, then, that, after his visits, Emily noted in her journal the way Lear's 'heavy post-happiness depression settled down on him' and that he felt happier at Farringford than anywhere else.

Lear's subsequent visits to the Isle of Wight in the 1860s were less than happy ones as he found the frequency of dinner parties and dances not to his taste; he also disliked the society of worship that was forming around Tennyson. Lear always preferred one-to-one conversations and found sycophancy distasteful. In particular, Lear found the newly arrived Julia Margaret Cameron overbearing and irritating. Moreover, Tennyson began to frustrate Lear, who recorded in his diary 'O would he were his poems'. In contrast, Lear idolised Emily:

> I should think, computing moderately, that fifteen angels, several hundreds of ordinary women, many philosophers, a heap of truly wise and kind mothers, three or four minor prophets and a lot of doctors and school-mistresses, might all be boiled down and yet their combined essence fall short of what Emily Tennyson really is...

During his 1860 visit, Lear mentioned one incident in which Tennyson exasperated him. Lear and Lushington were walking with the poet, when Tennyson saw local people approaching and refused to walk any further. Lear describes Tennyson as 'disagreeably querulous', owing to his insistence that they return home using an alternative route, along a particularly muddy path, to avoid the villagers coming from church. Lear wrote afterwards: 'believe this is my last visit to Farringford: -not can I wish it otherwise all things considered'.

One of Lear's other considerations was his dislike of Julia Margaret Cameron. Although at first Lear was eager to meet her, telling Emily in an 1855 letter, 'I cannot but say that I should have liked to see Mrs Cameron: which is vulgar, & savours curiosity', he changed his opinion once they met. During his 1860 visit, Lear was upset by the commotion and bother Cameron created and his feelings probably derive from one of the most recorded anecdotes associated with Tennyson's circle; one evening Cameron had eight men bring her grand piano from her house to Farringford, so that Lear could play it rather than Emily's inferior instrument. Although Emily records that Lear sang for a 'long time' that evening, she does not appear to have recognised Lear's exasperation with her neighbour. Of course, at this time Cameron did not make a great distinction between Farringford and Dimbola, and regarded the guests of one house as the guests also of the other. But Lear regarded her as the creator of 'odious incense palaver and fuss' and described Freshwater as having changed because her family had taken 'entire possession of the place - Camerons and Prinseps building everywhere'.

Nevertheless, Lear returned again in 1867 and noted the many changes that had taken place in the intervening years: the construction of a hotel, new houses and a new road. On this occasion, his hostility towards Tennyson increased and he criticised the poet's intolerance of and occasional harshness with his children, whom Lear adored. Lear wrote: 'AT snubs the boys in a brutal manner and is too sadly selfish sensual. I wonder how they are so respectful as they are, to a father so utterly wanting in self-respect as AT is'. In addition, Lear remained unhappy with Tennyson's behaviour toward Emily, having noted on a previous visit: 'I believe no other woman in all this world could live with him for a month. It always wrings me to leave Farringford, yet I doubt - as once before - whether I can go again'.

It was during his final visit to Farringford in 1869 that Lear was most exasperated by Tennyson. On one evening during Lear's stay, Tennyson expressed his uncertainty about whether to purchase two of Lear's illustrations of Corsica. The pair got into a heated argument, after which Lear decided to pack his bags. However, Emily intervened, convincing Tennyson to buy one of the pictures and persuading Lear to stay, and peace was made between the two men.

The last time Lear saw the Tennysons was at Aldworth in July 1877, and he described the visit as a happy one, noting that Emily looked well and that the poet was less disagreeable than before. For much of the 1870s and 1880s Lear lived aboard, identifying with the shipwrecked sailor in Tennyson's poem *Enoch Arden*. He settled in San Remo in 1871, first in Villa Emily and later in Villa Tennyson. The names of the homes reflect the affection he bore Emily but also the fact that he was working on illustrations and landscape drawings inspired by Tennyson's poems. Before his death, he collected these illustrations together and wrote a dedication to Emily, who had become 'Lady Emily' after her husband accepted a peerage in 1883. Shortly after his death, thirty-six of these engravings were published by Messers. Boussod, Valloden & Cowhich; however, the publisher only agreed to this if Tennyson would sign a hundred copies of the book. In his lifetime, Lear never achieved Tennyson's celebrity, which seemed to increase the value of everything it touched.

This c.1880 watercolour study is one of 200 illustrations Lear produced with the intention that they should accompany Tennyson's poems; it uses an isolated figure on a tropical island to depict Tennyson's shipwrecked Enoch Arden.

Lewis Carroll

Long before Lewis Carroll himself achieved literary fame as the author of *Alice's Adventures in Wonderland*, he was fascinated by Victorian celebrity and made concerted efforts to forge acquaintances with the best-known authors, artists and actors of his day. Often, he would seek introductions through well-connected friends, or the friends of friends; at other times, his talent for photography helped him to gain access to the homes of luminaries willing to have their portraits (or those of family members) taken. Carroll recorded many of his celebrity encounters in his diary, marking those he deemed to be of special importance with a 'white stone'. Notably, his first meetings with the Tennysons and, later, with Ellen Terry were commemorated in this way.

As a young man, Carroll (or, to give him his real name, Charles Lutwidge Dodgson) developed a profound regard for Tennyson's work. During his early years as a mathematics lecturer at Oxford's Christ Church College, he read *Maud* in a single day and described the canto beginning 'I have led her home' as 'true, passionate poetry'. Given this deep-seated admiration, it is not surprising to find that when the opportunity to meet his literary hero presented itself in September 1857 Carroll was quick to seize it. While holidaying in the Lake District, he discovered that the Tennysons were staying close by and decided to take a walk past their lodgings, 'intending,' as he wrote later in his diary, 'at least to see Tent Lodge (where Tennyson is staying) if not call'. Carroll adopts a deliberately casual tone in this retrospective account, suggesting that his main purpose in walking to Tent Lodge was to catch a glimpse of the house rather than its famous occupant; however, this version of events seems more than a little disingenuous for, on reaching the place, Carroll quickly resolved to take the liberty of calling, uninvited, on the Poet Laureate and his family. (Sceptical readers may suspect that this had been his plan all along.)

A couple of weeks earlier, Carroll had photographed Emily's young niece, Agnes, and this fortuitous prior acquaintance now acted as his passport into the Tennysons' holiday home. In his diary, Carroll reports:

> I sent in my [calling] card, adding (underneath the name) in pencil 'artist of "Agnes Grace"'.... On the strength of this introduction I was most kindly received and spent nearly an hour there. I also saw the two children, Hallam and Lionel, five and three years old, the most beautiful boys of their age I ever saw.

Disappointingly, Tennyson himself was not at home during the call so, before leaving, Carroll cannily created an opening for a second visit by requesting Emily's permission to photograph Hallam and Lionel at a future date. Emily agreed and even suggested that her husband might be persuaded to sit with them. Careful to preserve the appearance of modesty, Carroll wrote in his diary, 'I said I would not request [a sitting with Tennyson], as he must have refused so many that it is unfair to expect it'; nevertheless, he seems to have been excited by the prospect and returned to Tent Lodge only four days later.

This time Tennyson was present. Carroll described him as 'a strange shaggy-looking man', though kind and friendly, with 'a dry humour lurking in his style of talking'. Indeed, when Carroll brought out his portfolio of photographs after dinner, the Laureate is reported to have amused the assembled company with his witty remarks about the expressions captured in the portraits. The evening was a 'most delightful' one for Carroll: the Tennysons were so complimentary about his work that he retained 'strong hopes of ultimately getting a sitting from the poet'. These hopes were to be fulfilled a week later, when he again called on the Tennysons, this time at their friends the Marshalls', with his photographic equipment in tow. Though Carroll's diary account of the day is curiously understated—'I got pictures of Mr. and Mrs. Tennyson, Hallam, Mr. Lushington (a friend of Mr. Tennyson's), and a group of Hallam, Lionel and Mr. Marshall's little girl Julia'—one can imagine his sense of satisfaction at finally having photographed England's notoriously publicity-shy Laureate.

Carroll again made efforts to integrate himself into Tennyson's circle while holidaying on the Isle of Wight in 1859. By this time, he seems to have gained a reputation as something of a 'lion-hunter', or relentless pursuer of celebrities—a reputation he was keen to disavow. In a letter to his cousin, he wrote, rather defensively:

Wilfred must have basely misrepresented me if he said that I followed the Laureate down to his retreat, as I went, not knowing that he was there, to stay with an old college friend at Freshwater. Being there, I had the inalienable right of a freeborn Briton to make a morning call, which I did, in spite of my friend Collyns having assured me that the Tennysons had not yet arrived. There was a man painting the garden railing when I walked up to the house, of whom I asked if Mr. Tennyson were at home, fully expecting the answer 'No,' so that it was an agreeable surprise when he said, 'He's there, sir,' and pointed him out...not many yards off, mowing his lawn.

It is interesting to note that Carroll represents this visit to Farringford in very much the same vein as he represented his first visit to Tent Lodge, claiming, in both cases, to have had no preconceived notion of meeting with the Tennysons. Whether we believe his protestations or not, we have to admire his audacity; following on from this latest unsolicited call, Carroll was rewarded with an invitation to take tea at Farringford that evening and to dine there the next day.

Over the course of several summers spent on the Isle of Wight, Carroll also secured introductions to some of the other members of Tennyson's circle, including the Camerons and the Taylors. However, he never really achieved great popularity with the Freshwater celebrities, nor did he ever manage to integrate himself fully into their group. Julia Margaret Cameron, of course, treated him with her customary generosity, inviting him to spend several evenings at her family's home, but the two disagreed on the matter of photography. After Cameron organised a joint exhibition of their work at Dimbola, the punctilious Carroll wrote a letter to his sister dismissing his hostess's photographs as 'all taken purposely out of focus'; some he even described as 'hideous'. As for the Tennysons, Carroll seems to have enjoyed a closer friendship with Hallam and Lionel than with Alfred and Emily. Whereas the boys took great pleasure in Carroll's company, the Laureate seems to have found him mildly irritating and to have absented himself for long periods during Carroll's visits. In fact, the socially awkward Carroll was always most comfortable around children, having an unfortunate tendency to rub adults up the wrong way. Famously, the elder Tennysons were moved to cut off their acquaintance with him after he wrote to them in 1870 asking for permission to read and circulate a copy of 'The Window' (an unpublished poem by Tennyson) that had come into his possession. Emily's reply was curt and to the point: 'It is useless troubling Mr. Tennyson with a request which will only revive the annoyance he has already had on the subject (of unauthorised works coming into the public domain).... A gentleman should understand that when an author does not give his works to the public he has his own reasons for it'. Unsurprisingly, their relationship never really recovered, although Carroll continued to take an interest in the Tennyson children, writing in 1872 to recommend a system for the treatment of Lionel's stammer.

One member of Freshwater circle with whom Carroll did enjoy a genuine friendship was Ellen Terry (though, like so many of his personal relationships, it was far from uncomplicated). Carroll had taken a keen interest in Terry ever since seeing her perform the role of Mamillius in *The Winter's Tale* aged nine and made repeated attempts to engineer a meeting with her during her adolescence. In 1862, he wrote in his diary, with perceptible frustration, 'All my photographic victims seem to be available but the Terrys [Ellen and her sister, Kate], who are acting in Bristol'. In July 1864, he visited Little Holland House on the invitation of Sara Prinsep and met with G. F. Watts but, to his disappointment, the painter's young wife was not present. A couple of months later, the playwright Tom Taylor gave Carroll a note of introduction to Terry's parents; however, each time Carroll visited their London home, Ellen was away. He finally got to meet her on 21 December 1864, eight years after he had first admired her performance in *The Winter's Tale*:

In the [Terry's] drawing-room I found Miss Kate Terry, Florence, and to my delight, the one I have always most wished to meet of the family, Mrs. Watts [Ellen Terry]....I was very much pleased with what I saw of [her]—lively and pleasant, almost childish in her fun, but perfectly ladylike.

Carroll's admiration for Terry developed into a full-blown friendship; sadly, though, this was not to last. When, separated from but still married to Watts, Terry moved in with the architect and designer Edward Godwin and bore him two children, Carroll cut off all correspondence with her. He only renewed their friendship when Terry again became 'respectable' in his eyes, following her marriage to the actor Charles Wardell in 1877. 'All the sad past is now, one may hope, passed for ever, and I am only too glad

This 1856 photograph shows Charles Lutwidge Dodgson, who would later find fame as 'Lewis Carroll', author of *Alice's Adventures in Wonderland*. Copyright of Surrey History Centre

to forget it, and to rejoice in her present position as a wife,' he wrote to a mutual friend, rather condescendingly, following their reacquaintance. Carroll was, undoubtedly, a complex man, full of contradictions. Judgmental of others, he resented being judged himself and while he had no qualms about soliciting autographs or photographic portraits from famous Victorians (in ways that could, at times, be deemed rather pushy), he refused to indulge his own autograph - or photograph-collecting fans. He explained,

> My constant aim is to remain, personally, unknown to the world; consequently I have always refused applications for photographs or autographs, as my features and handwriting belong to me as a private individual—and I often beg even my own private friends, who possess one or the other, not to put them into albums where strangers can see them.

In this light, Carroll's adoption of a pseudonym can be seen as an attempt to separate and protect his private self from his public, literary identity. Nevertheless, following the publication of the *Alice* books, he often received letters from eager fans convinced that Charles Dodgson and Lewis Carroll were one and the same. By the 1890s, these letters had become so frequent that he went to the trouble of printing a leaflet (The Stranger Circular) denying any connection with books not bearing the Dodgson name, which could be forwarded to bothersome correspondents. A lioniser who detested being lionised, an indefatigable fan fiercely protective of his own privacy, Lewis Carroll epitomised the ambivalence of celebrity in the Victorian age.

The Royal Family

The Tennysons and the Camerons were by no means the only famous nineteenth-century families to have fallen for the charms of the Isle of Wight. Queen Victoria and her husband, Prince Albert, were also captivated by the island's beauty and seclusion and, in 1845, they purchased Osborne House, located just outside East Cowes, as a holiday retreat. With its superb views across the Solent, elegant Italianate buildings and beautiful terraced gardens, Osborne was to become one of the Queen's favourite residences; she enthused that 'it is impossible to imagine a prettier spot' and spent many happy summers and Christmases there, surrounded by her family.

Farringford lay just over fifteen miles away from Osborne, yet there was no social communication between the Queen and her Poet Laureate during his family's early years on the Isle of Wight. This situation was to change rather suddenly in 1856. One bright spring day, Prince Albert decided to drop in on the Tennysons, unannounced. Under ordinary circumstances, this house-call would have been a welcome surprise; as it turned out, the Prince could hardly have picked a less opportune moment for his first visit. The Tennysons had recently bought Farringford and were in the process of renovating and redecorating the place. Consequently, the house was in a state of upheaval, with a jumble of furniture and half-unpacked boxes lining the corridors. One can only imagine Emily's feelings on hearing that, in the midst of all this commotion, she was expected to receive a Royal guest! Her journal gives some sense of the disorder that greeted Prince Albert's arrival:

> 13th May 1856 - In the midst of all our confusion, while all imaginable things strewed the drawing room and the bookshelves were bare and the chairs and tables dancing, Prince Albert came. He had driven over suddenly from Osborne. The parlour-maid went to the front door, heard the Prince's name announced and being bewildered by the confusion in the house and not knowing what to do with 'His Royal Highness' stood stock still....

In spite of this rather inauspicious start, the Royal visit appears ultimately to have been a success. In a letter to her sister, Emily reported that the Prince was 'very kind, shook hands with Ally [Alfred] and talked to him very gaily.' Indeed, Albert seems to have reacted to the chaos around him with impeccable good humour, declaring Farringford to be such a 'pretty place' that he would 'certainly bring the Queen to see it.' The Tennysons spent the next few days in a state of anxious anticipation, awaiting Her Majesty's arrival; however, possibly owing to bad weather, the projected visit never took place. Tennyson would have to wait a little while longer for his first private interview with Victoria.

In the meantime, Prince Albert continued to take a keen interest in England's Laureate. He was an ardent admirer of Tennyson's poetry - so much so that in 1860 he wrote to Farringford, requesting that Tennyson sign his copy of *Idylls of the King*.

Buckingham Palace
17th May 1860

My dear Mr Tennyson
Will you forgive me if I intrude on your leisure with a request which I have thought some little time of making, viz. that you would be good enough to write your name in the accompanying volume of your 'Idylls of the King'? You would thus add a peculiar interest to the book, containing those beautiful songs, from the perusal of which I derived the greatest enjoyment. They quite rekindle the feeling with which the legends of King Arthur must have inspired the chivalry of old, whilst the graceful form in which they are presented blends those feelings with the softer tone of our present age.
Believe me always yours truly,
Albert

Tennyson, usually so reluctant to indulge the demands of bothersome autograph-hunters, was in this case happy to oblige!

Queen Victoria, like her husband, held Tennyson's poetry in high regard. It was following the death of her beloved Albert in 1861, however, that the Laureate's words came to acquire a special meaning for her. Absorbed by grief, she sought solace in the stanzas of *In Memoriam*, Tennyson's moving tribute to his own much-missed friend Arthur Henry Hallam. 'Only those who have suffered as I do, can understand these beautiful poems,' the Queen confided in her diary. She also found consolation in the 'Dedication' to the Prince Consort that was added to the *Idylls of the King* shortly after his death. The Queen's daughter, Princess Alice, wrote that 'Mr Alfred Tennyson could not have chosen a more beautiful or true testimonial to the memory of him who was so really good and noble', noting that his lines had helped to soothe her mother's 'aching, bleeding heart' during those first painful months of mourning.

The Queen's sense of affinity with Tennyson's poetry led her to request a personal meeting with the Laureate at Osborne in the spring of 1862. A notoriously shy man, Tennyson was more than a little nervous at the prospect and afterwards could recollect little of what had been said to him. The Queen's impressions of the meeting were clearer: in her diary, she described Tennyson as a 'peculiar looking', 'oddly dressed' man, but one who was 'full of unbounded appreciation of beloved Albert'. Indeed, Tennyson seems at one point to have been visibly moved by thoughts of the Prince's demise: 'when he spoke of my own loss, of that to the Nation, his eyes quite filled with tears,' the Queen recalled approvingly.

Over the next thirty years, the friendship between Tennyson and Queen Victoria continued to grow. As Poet Laureate, Tennyson was of course obliged to take an interest in the monarchy and matters of state—part of his role was to compose poems commemorating Royal marriages, births, deaths and so on—but his relationship with his Sovereign seems to have been marked by a genuine sense of warmth, respect and fellow-feeling. Tennyson regularly sent copies of his new works to the Queen; she, in turn, sent Tennyson gifts—books and photographs with handwritten inscriptions—as tokens of her regard and, on a number of occasions, invited his family to call on her at Osborne. After her first visit to the Royal residence in May 1863, Emily wrote in her journal, 'I never met a Lady with whom I could talk so easily and never felt so little shy with any stranger after the first few minutes....One feels that the Queen is a woman to live and die for'. Though Victoria famously remained in mourning for Albert throughout her life, the Tennysons did not find the mood at Osborne overly sombre or oppressive. Emily reported that the Queen 'laughed heartily at many things that were said' and, on one occasion, was particularly amused by Tennyson's grumblings about 'the Cockneys' (day-trippers) who laid siege to Farringford each summer, hoping to get a glimpse of its famous owner. The Queen's observation, 'we are not much troubled by them here,' prompted a typically gruff reply from the Laureate: 'Perhaps I should not be either, Your Majesty, if I could stick a sentry at my gates.'

In later years, as Tennyson was increasingly troubled by poor health, meetings with the Queen inevitably became less frequent. Nevertheless, the two kept up a regular, personal correspondence and the Royal Family maintained their love for Tennyson's work. The Queen's children often entertained themselves at Osborne by staging tableaux vivants of famous scenes from the *Idylls of the King* and, on a couple of occasions, they invited the poet's eldest son, Hallam, along to witness their performances. The continued intimacy between the two families meant that Victoria was one of the first to be informed of Tennyson's death on the morning of 6th October 1892. The Queen, who was staying at Balmoral in Scotland at the time, swiftly telegraphed her condolences to Hallam and Emily, describing herself as 'truly deeply grieved' by the news. It is in her personal diary, however, that we can best gain a sense of the great admiration she felt for the man whose poetry had so comforted her during her long widowhood:

> October 6, 1892 - I heard that dear old Ld Tennyson had breathed his last, a great national loss.... What beautiful lines he wrote to me for my darling Albert, and for my children and Eddy. He died with his hand on his Shakespeare, and the moon shining full into the window, and over him. A worthy end to such a remarkable man.

An extract from Prince Albert's 1860 letter to Tennyson, in which he asks the Laureate to autograph his copy of *Idylls of the King*.

Tennyson's death

By the time of Tennyson's death, the circle that had formed around him on the Isle of Wight was all but dissolved: Cameron and Lear were dead and Terry, Carroll and Watts were no longer in close contact with each other. Nothing in his life proved Tennyson's celebrity as his death did. Tennyson's stature as a great but also beloved poet was confirmed by his public funeral - something usually reserved for statesmen or war heroes - and his burial at Westminster Abbey and the placement of his bust in Poets' Corner. The newspaper coverage of Tennyson's death and its aftermath underlined not only Tennyson's place in British public life but also the power of his celebrity to bring the British people together in a show of grief and mourning. For the commentators, his death marked the end of a golden age of poetry, and they described him as the last of the Romantic poets and used his poems, in particular, *In Memoriam,* as a means of expressing national grief. Tennyson's death-bed image, showing him clutching his Shakespeare, was published in many illustrated journals and magazines, and the poet was compared to the character of King Arthur from his *Idylls of the King.* Everyone was encouraged to catch a last glimpse of the reclusive poet, who in his death had become finally the nation's possession, a saint-like figure available to be venerated. Journalists captured and exacerbated public grief, suggesting that their readers should attend the funeral, not least of all to see which Victorian celebrities would be present. According to Edmund Gosse, the funeral was a chaotic affair involving a scramble for seats and 'a crowd of perfectly callous nonentities, treating the thing as a show and rather a poor one.' While the whole spectacle of the funeral would have horrified Tennyson, it confirmed his position not only as a popular and critically acclaimed poet, but also as a celebrity. No subsequent poet has come close, or perhaps would wish to come close, to achieving this feat.

A REMINISCENCE: THE LATE LORD TENNYSON AND HIS NURSE ON FRESHWATER DOWNS

A SKETCH FROM LIFE

Following Tennyson's death, many Victorian periodicals published special commemorative issues. This edition of the *Graphic* carried a full-page portrait of Tennyson, walking on High Down, on its front cover.

Illustrations

p. 2—*Illustrated London News*, 23 April 1864. Special Collections and Archives, Cardiff University Library.

p. 5—'The Dirty Monk' (Alfred, Lord Tennyson) photograph by Julia Margaret Cameron 1865. The Julia Margaret Cameron Trust, Dimbola.

p. 6—Albumen print of Alfred and Emily Tennyson and their sons Hallam and Lionel, by Oscar Rejlander, 1863. Copyright Reading Museum (Reading Borough Council). All rights reserved.

p. 8—Portrait of Lady Emily Tennyson by George Frederick Watts, 1862. The COLLECTION: Art and Archaeology in Lincolnshire (Usher Gallery, Lincoln).

p. 9—Alfred Tennyson, 1st Baron Tennyson by George Frederic Watts, 1863-1864. © National Portrait Gallery, London.

p. 11—Map of Freshwater. The Isle of Wight Record Office.

p. 11—Farringford, South Side by Edward Lear, 1864. Tennyson Research Centre, Lincolnshire County Council.

p. 13—'The May Queen' from *Idylls of the King*, photograph by Julia Margaret Cameron, 1874. The Julia Margaret Cameron Trust, Dimbola.

p. 14— Julia Margaret Cameron with her two children, Henry Herschel Hay and Charlie Hay by Unknown photographer, 1858. © National Portrait Gallery, London.

p. 14—'The Whisper of the Muse', photograph by Julia Margaret Cameron, 1865. © Victoria and Albert Museum, London.

p. 16—Self-portrait of G.F. Watts in Middle Age, 1879. Watts Galley, Compton, Surrey.

p. 17— Dame (Alice) Ellen Terry ('Choosing') by George Frederic Watts, 1864. © National Portrait Gallery, London.

p. 20—Edward Lear, photograph by Schier and Schoefft, 1866-1867. © National Portrait Gallery, London.

p. 20—Letter to Alfred Tennyson from Edward Lear, 27 June 1864. Tennyson Research Centre, Lincolnshire County Council.

p. 21—'Enoch Arden's Island' by Edward Lear, c. 1880. Tennyson Research Centre, Lincolnshire County Council.

p. 24— Photograph of Charles Lutwidge Dodgson, 1856. Reproduced by permission of Surrey History Centre.

p. 26—Letter to Alfred Tennyson from Prince Albert, 17 May 1860. Tennyson Research Centre, Lincolnshire County Council.

p. 27—*The Graphic*, 15 October 1892. Special Collections and Archives, Cardiff University Library.

Selected Bibliography

Nina Auerbach, *Ellen Terry: Player in her Time*, New York: W.W. Norton, 1987.

Wilfrid Blunt, *England's Michelangelo: A Biography of George Frederic Watts*, London: Hamish Hamilton, 1975.

Briddon's Illustrated Handbook to the Isle of Wight, Containing Everything Necessary to the Tourist, Ryde: J. Briddon, 1862.

Jim Cheshire, ed., *Tennyson Transformed: Alfred Lord Tennyson and Visual Culture*, Farnam: Lund Humphries, 2009.

Morton N. Cohen, ed., *The Letters of Lewis Carroll*, London: Macmillan, 1979.

———. Ed., *Lewis Carroll: A Biography*, New York: Alfred A. Knopf, 1995.

Julian Cox, ed., *In Focus: Julia Margaret Cameron*, Los Angeles: J. Paul Getty Museum, 1996.

Julian Cox and Colin Ford, *Julia Margaret Cameron: The Complete Photographs*, London: Thames & Hudson, 2003.

Edith Craig and Christopher St. John, eds., *Ellen Terry's Memoirs*, London: Victor Gollancz, 1933.

Hope Dyson and Charles Tennyson, eds., *Dear and Honoured Lady: The Correspondence between Queen Victoria and Alfred Tennyson*, London: Macmillan, 1969.

Eric Eisner, *Nineteenth-Century Poetry and Literary Celebrity*, London: Palgrave Macmillan, 2009.

Edith Nicholl Ellison, *A Child's Recollections of Tennyson*, London: J. Dent, 1907.

Colin Ford, *Julia Margaret Cameron: A Critical Biography*, Los Angeles: J. Paul Getty Museum, 2003.

Hester Thackeray Fuller, *Three Freshwater Friends: Tennyson, Watts and Mrs. Cameron*, Newport: Isle of Wight County Press, 1933.

Edmund Gosse, *Portraits and Sketches: The Collected Essays of Edmund Gosse*, London: Heinemann, 1913.

Veronica Franklin Gould, *G. F. Watts: The Last Great Victorian*, New Haven: Yale University Press, 2004.

Roger Lancelyn Green, ed., *The Diaries of Lewis Carroll*, Westport: Greenwood Press, 1971.

Violet Hamilton, *Annals of my Glass House: Photographs by Julia Margaret Cameron*, Seattle and London: Ruth Chandler Williamson Gallery, 1996.

Brian Hinton, *Immortal Faces: Julia Margaret Cameron on the Isle of Wight*, Newport: Isle of Wight County Press, 1992.

James O. Hoge, ed., *The Letters of Emily Lady Tennyson*, University Park: Pennsylvania State University Press, 1974.

———. Ed., *Lady Tennyson's Journal*, Charlottesville: University Press of Virginia, 1981.

Amanda Hopkinson, *Julia Margaret Cameron*, London: Virago Press, 1986.

Richard J. Hutchings and Brian Hinton, eds. *The Farringford Journals of Emily Tennyson 1853-1864*, Newport, Isle of Wight County Press, 1986.

Cecil Y. Lang and Edgar F. Shannon, Jr., eds, *The Letters of Alfred Lord Tennyson*, vol. II 1851-1870, Oxford: Clarendon Press, 1987.

Kathryn Ledbetter, *Tennyson and Victorian Periodicals: Commodities in Context*, Aldershot: Ashgate, 2007.

Robert Bernard Martin, *Tennyson, The Unquiet Heart*, London: Faber and Faber, 1980.

Samantha Matthews, *Poetical Remains· Poets' Graves, Bodies, and Books in the Nineteenth Century*, Oxford: Oxford University Press, 2004.

Tom Mole, *Byron's Romantic Celebrity: Industrial Culture and the Hermeneutic of Intimacy*, Basingstoke: Palgrave Macmillan, 2007.

George G. Napier, *The Homes and Haunts of Alfred Lord Tennyson*, Glasgow: J. Maclehose, 1892.

Vivian Noakes, ed, *Edward Lear; Selected Letters*, Oxford: Clarendon Press, 1988.

———. Ed., *Edward Lear 1812-1888*, London: Royal Academy of Arts, 1985.

———. *Edward Lear: Life of a Wanderer*, Gloucester: Sutton Publishing Ltd, 2004.

Victoria Olsen, *From Life: Julia Margaret Cameron and Victorian Photography*, London: Aurum Press, 2003.

Leonée Ormond, *Alfred Lord Tennyson: A Literary Life*, London: Macmillan, 1993.

Norman Page, ed., *Tennyson: Interviews and Recollections*, London, Macmillan, 1983.

Hester Ritchie, ed., *Letters of Anne Thackeray Ritchie*, London: Albemarle Street, W., 1924.

Alfred Lord Tennyson, *The Works of Alfred Lord Tennyson*, Ware: Wordsworth, 1994.

Charles Tennyson, *Farringford: Home of Alfred Lord Tennyson*, Lincoln, Tennyson Society, 1976.

Hallam Tennyson, *Alfred Lord Tennyson: A Memoir.* 2 vols., London, Macmillan, 1898.

Ann Thwaite, *Emily Tennyson: The Poet's Wife*, London, Faber and Faber, 1996.

Lynne Truss, *Tennyson and his Circle*, London: National Portrait Gallery, 1999.

J. Redding Ware, *The Isle of Wight*, London: Provost & Co., 1869.

Mary Seton Watts, *George Frederic Watts: The Annuals of an Artist's Life*, 3 vols., London, Macmillan, 1912.

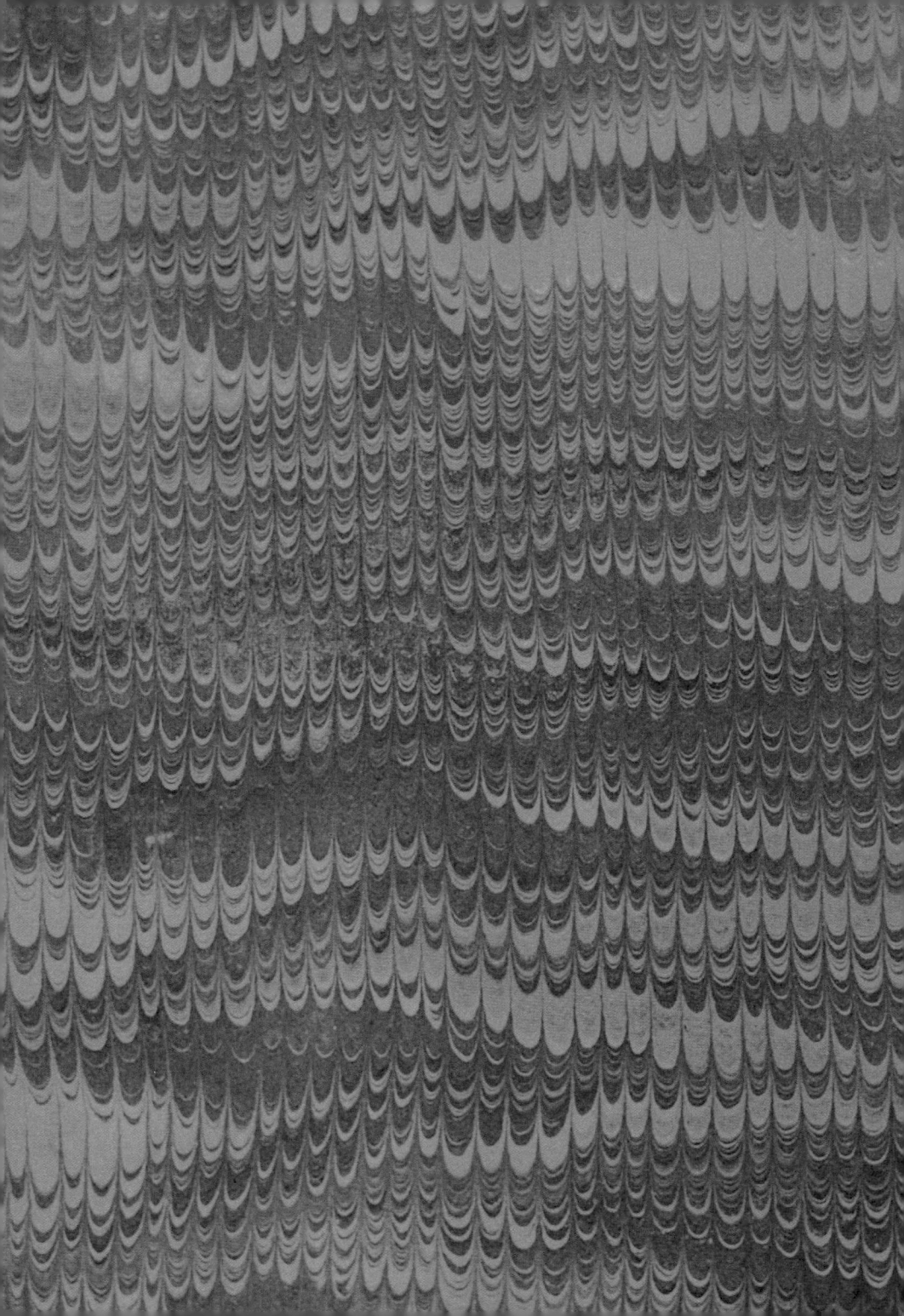